The Great
Kite Fight

Rob Waring, *Series Editor*

HEINLE
CENGAGE Learning™

Australia • Brazil • Japan • Korea • Mexico • Singapore • Spain • United Kingdom • United States

Words to Know

This story is set in the country of Japan. It takes place in the northern part, in the city of Shirone [ʃirouneɪ].

A **The Big Kite Festival.** Read the definitions. Then complete the paragraph with the correct forms of the words.

battle: a fight between two forces or groups
enthusiastic: having an energetic interest in something
festival: a public holiday or celebration
kite: a light wooden framework covered with paper and flown
maniac: a person who acts crazy; a madman

This story is about a five-day (1)_____ in the northern part of Japan. During the celebration, teams of people fly (2)_____ over a river. The competition also involves (3)_____ between teams in which they try to force each other's kites out of the air. The teams become so (4)_____ about kites that some people call them 'Kite Crazy.' Others consider them to be (5)_____ who can't control themselves during the event!

A Tug of War

B **Tug of War.** Read the paragraph. Then complete the definitions with the correct words or phrases.

At the Shirone kite festival, a tug of war starts after one team has pulled another team's kite out of the air. During this part of the competition, the two rivals pull on ropes to determine which team is stronger. Each team clings to their kite ropes and pulls as hard as possible. Their goal is to capture the other team's kite by breaking the ropes that hold it. These clashes are a thrilling part of the contest and everyone fights fiercely until the end.

1. A c_____ is similar to a heated argument or fight.
2. Another word for 'enemy' is r_____.
3. To c_____ is to hold on tightly to something.
4. To c_____ is to take something by force.
5. A competition which involves pulling ropes in opposite directions is a t_____ o_____ w_____.

Once a year, the people of Shirone, Japan, leave their quiet lives behind them and begin preparing for an activity about which they are absolutely **passionate**.[1] At this time of year, they become so enthusiastic about a competition, that local residents have given the condition a name. They call it *Tako Kichi:* Kite Crazy.

Kazuo Tamura,[2] a local resident and kite-flying fan, explains what 'Kite Crazy' means. "Kite Crazy refers to people who really love kites," he says. "People who think more about kites than getting their three meals a day. Even when they go to bed, they can't fall asleep because they see kites flying over their beds." Sleeplessness? Kites flying over beds? What is it about kite flying that makes the residents of Shirone so crazy?

---

[1] **passionate:** feeling very strongly about something
[2] **Kazuo Tamura:** [kɑzuoʊ tɑmʊɔrɑ]

🎧 CD 2, Track 05

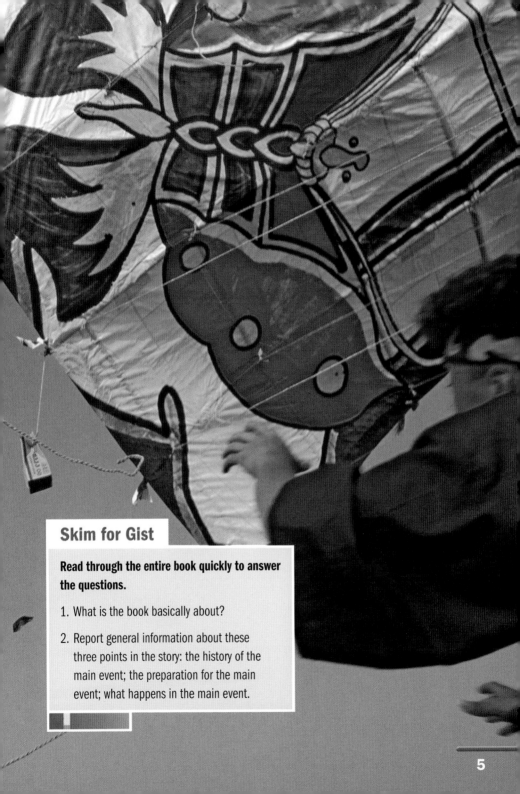

Skim for Gist

Read through the entire book quickly to answer the questions.

1. What is the book basically about?

2. Report general information about these three points in the story: the history of the main event; the preparation for the main event; what happens in the main event.

Normally Shirone is a quiet and peaceful place, like many other towns that are found in northern Japan. Farmers work hard through the spring to plant their rice on time, but when the work is done, they turn their attention away from the earth. They emerge from their labors ready to have some fun and join in a five-day festival that celebrates the open sky—the Great Shirone Kite Fight.

The Great Kite Fight is not a new event, but part of an old tradition that began 250 years ago. Several older paintings are still in existence which feature past great kite battles as their subject matter. These historic pieces serve to illustrate the beginnings of the festival. The kite fighting tradition actually originated from an ancient legend. According to the story, a giant kite was given to a village leader by the local **lord**.[3] The kite was so huge that it damaged houses and **crops**[4] in the fields when it unexpectedly came crashing down. Soon after, villagers who were angry or upset with each other started using kites to resolve their disagreements. The one who won the kite battle also won the argument. Eventually, these battles evolved into a festival where people could have their battles in the sky and rid themselves of a bit of stress every spring. For a growing number of passionate kite flyers, this annual kite fight became a prime opportunity for some 'high-level' enjoyment.

---

[3]**lord:** a man of high social status
[4]**crop:** plants or grains grown in large quantities

These days, the kite festival is as popular as it ever was. Now, as with previous years, kite madness comes to Shirone every June, and it affects people of all ages. Residents both old and young join the fun and just about anybody who can cling to a piece of kite rope gets involved. The town itself is transformed into the equivalent of a giant kite factory as rival teams prepare for battle. Playgrounds, parking lots, the driveways of houses, and even schools become work areas for the teams. The kite makers occupy almost every inch of free space available in order to make their huge and fantastic creations.

Kazuo Tamura is an internationally known kite-flying team leader. He feels that the kite festival is not only significant for him but also for the entire town and society as well. He explains in his own words: "This event is very important to me. It's not just a question of having a good time. Somehow, underneath a sky that's full of kites, everyone seems equal." Tamura's beliefs about the benefits of the Kite Fight don't stop there. He also feels that there's a peaceful element to the event as well, "No one flies a kite in times of war. So the festival is like a sign that we're at peace."

The festival kites of Shirone come in all shapes and sizes. However, they all have one thing in common; they are made by hand and put together carefully and precisely in the traditional way. The teams must be able to cooperate well in order to make the kites, and spend many hours designing, constructing, and painting their creations. Each of the kites has a distinct colorful design as well. Some of them have faces, some have simple designs, and others have complex patterns that require a considerable amount of time and effort. Every team has its own specialist painter who works for weeks to capture the special look that symbolizes and identifies their particular team.

Finally, the opening day of the festival arrives. One thousand five hundred kites are designed, decorated, and ready to be flown. Slowly, the teams gather to celebrate and get the festival started. Then, they proudly **parade**[5] their newly made kites through the streets of the town on their way to the battleground of the Great Kite Fight. As marching bands play and people shout excitedly, the town gets its first look at this year's creations. The biggest kites are called *odako*. They are difficult and uncomfortable to carry and are not easy to get into the air, but 13 different teams have come to try their best to fly them. Other teams prefer the smaller kites called *rokako*, which are much easier to move through the air. One could consider them to be more like **fighter jets**[6] whereas the *odako* are more like **heavy bombers**.[7] If it all sounds a little bit like war, that's because it is; the members of these teams are here to battle, dominate, and win!

---

[5]**parade *(verb)*:** display proudly
[6]**fighter jet:** a small, fast plane that fights in the air
[7]**heavy bomber:** a large plane that drops bombs and other weapons

For centuries, the battle of the kites has taken place along Shirone's central river, the **Nakanokuchi**.[8] The competing teams, dressed in traditional clothing, stand on opposite sides of the river as they plan and prepare to gain the best position. This long-standing tradition really is like a battle in a war. The goal is for one team to capture another team's kite by using their own kite and rope. The teams try to wrap the rope from their kite around the ropes of the rival team's kite. They then try to use their physical power to pull the rival's kite from the sky. Lots of loud shouting and cries of excitement can be heard as the teams try to capture the other teams' kites. It's an extremely thrilling time, both for the participants and the spectators.

Once one team has captured another team's kite, however, that's not the end of the battle; it is time for the real competition to begin. Once both kites are down, the ropes remain **twisted**[9] together and the kites can't be separated until one team drops their rope. The teams must desperately cling to their kite ropes, doing everything they can to keep their grip. Remember, the teams are located on the opposite sides of a river, so the first team to drop or break its rope will lose the battle and the kites will fall into the water. Therefore, these tugs of war often continue fiercely to the finish. Each team member must show strength of both mind and body as they try to pull the rival team members down so that they can no longer hang on to their kite.

---

[8] **Nakanokuchi:** [nɑkɑnoʊktʃi]
[9] **twist:** bring together by making a circular motion

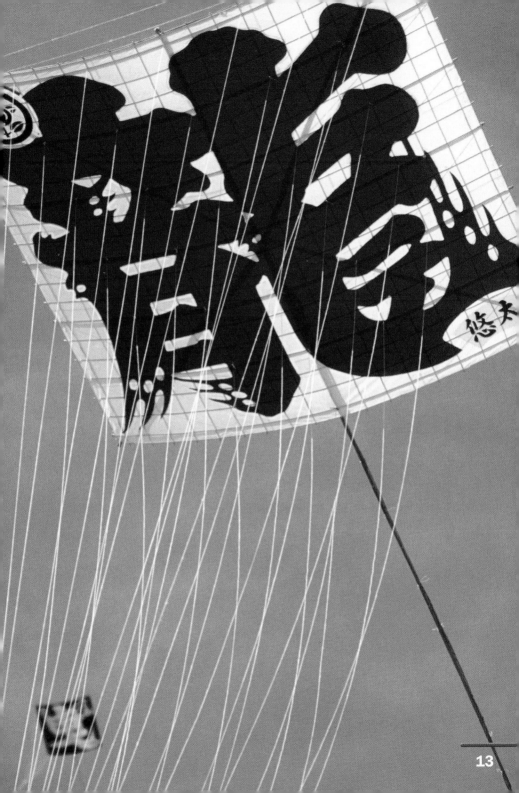

Unfortunately, in the tug of war between the teams, both of the kites are twisted, pulled, and basically destroyed. These kite battles often carry on for a considerable length of time, and usually leave people wondering, which team will win and which will lose. Nobody knows, but it's certainly a thrilling fight. Finally, when one team's rope breaks—usually after lots of pulling and hard work—a winner is declared. Extra points are given to the winning side for every inch of rope it captures from the losing team, and the points are recorded on a score board at the side of the river. It is obviously a competition which the locals take very seriously, but no matter who wins, there is always something lost. This become obvious as both teams' kites are left floating in the river, wet masses of paper and wood that were once the pride of the local teams.

All along the river, teams get involved in clashes that quickly lead to open war. The battles spread to the town, and almost everyone gets involved. Teams of children fight bravely against each other as the power of the wind nearly pulls them off their feet. At one point, the fighting gets so involved that the police must step in. No, not to break up a fight, but to help a group of kite fighters to cross the railway tracks! The policeman holds the team back with a stop gesture, and then finally, when the train has passed and the crossing is safe, the battle continues. The team races down the street, desperately fighting to capture the rival kite. The whole town seems to have gone mad; kite craziness is more than just an illness during the Great Kite Fight—it becomes an **epidemic!**[10]

---

[10]**epidemic:** a disease that spreads very quickly among many people

Scan for Information

Scan pages 17 and 18 to find the information.

1. Why are some kite fighters disappointed at the end of day one?

2. What kind of wind do the larger kites need?

3. What does Tamura think is the most important factor for teams?

By the end of day one, thousands of the smaller kites have been destroyed, but not everyone has been able to enjoy the competition. The large *odako* kites are still not flying. Unfortunately, the teams cannot even get the huge *odakos* into the air. The wind has been blowing from the east, and without a stable northern wind, the larger kites are helpless. They're simply too big for the wind to lift into the air. When one team tries to get theirs off the ground, it rises for a short period of time, and then falls slowly to the earth, catching itself on a building on the way down and tearing as it falls.

The *odako* teams must wait for a change in the weather, and hope that they are ready when the north wind finally arrives. While they are waiting, the teams step back from the excitement of the riverside to work on their ropes, ensuring that they are strung, or put together, correctly. The ropes used in the Shirone kite fights are made by hand, which makes them extremely strong. Very tough ropes are essential to Shirone kites because they have two purposes: first, they control the kite, and secondly they have to be able to stand up to the fierce and **aggressive**[11] tugs of war.

_____

[11] **aggressive:** determined; forcefully done

Each team keeps their own method of making their ropes strong a strict secret. This secrecy is part of the competitiveness and teamwork that constitutes an important part of the kite festival. In fact, many believe that without teamwork, there might be no festival at all.

Kazuo Tamura explains what competing in the kite festival is like, stating that working together is of the greatest importance. "The most important thing is teamwork," he says. "Everyone runs around clinging to the same rope, so they have to work together. This is very important. Without teamwork, these kites won't fly; they'll fall right to the ground."

Tamura's plan for teamwork is a good one, but even the best teamwork doesn't matter if there is no wind to fly the kites. A second *odako* kite tries to make it up in the air only to fail. As it falls to the side of the river, it catches on the side of the bridge and is damaged. By the third day of this five-day festival, there is still no northern wind, and everyone is very disappointed. They all wish that the wind would pick up, but it doesn't help.

The *odako* teams are worried that this may be the first year in Shirone's history that they will not have a chance to fight; but they aren't giving up on the fun. When evening falls, the *odako* teams still manage to have a good time and celebrate the festival. They spend the evening dancing in the darkness, singing, and playing instruments. Everyone welcomes the break from the stress of the kite competition; moreover, they welcome an opportunity to relax and have a little fun. After all, that is what the five-day festival is all about for most people, giving themselves a chance to go a little crazy.

On the fifth and final day of the competition, the wind continues to deliver disappointment, but at the last minute something wonderful happens. With just one hour remaining in the event, a northern wind comes down along the river. At last, the oversized kites are released from their earthly imprisonment and lifted up into the sky. The crowds shout with happiness as the beautiful, giant *odako* kites rise high into the air at last. Now, finally, Kazuo Tamura's team will have its only chance to win a tug of war before the festival ends. It's a situation that requires both skill and passion; luckily Tamura's team has plenty of both. Tamura shouts loudly as he races down the side of the river to get his team ready. The entire group must be both excited and motivated to win.

At last, the two rival kites are lifted up into the air by the soft wind and they begin dancing slowly across the sky. As they do, the rope from one of the kites begins to wrap itself around the rope of the other. Suddenly, the two kites are wound together and go crashing towards the river. The young men on Tamura's team have managed to capture the competing team's kite and Tamura goes wild with excitement. Acting as both teacher and coach, he yells and encourages the team to work harder as the next part of the competition begins. Several meters of twisted rope lie across the river, connecting the two teams in a fierce tug of war. For the teams, the battle seems more like a matter of life and death—not just a kite competition!

The clash between the two opposing teams of kite fighters continues for quite some time. Both teams seem confident of a victory, but the results are still unsure and the battle is in full force. After a while, the teams switch techniques and start shaking the ropes up and down, hoping that maybe the weight of the kites will cause their rival's rope to break. All the while that the teams are battling, Tamura runs around his team, shouting like a madman, and cheering nonstop. One can easily see why people could say that he has gone completely Kite Crazy, but Tamura doesn't think he's all that crazy. He simply considers himself to be a big fan of the sport. "People call me a kite maniac," Tamura says, laughing. "I am a kite enthusiast. That's just me," he argues. "They call me a kite maniac, but I don't think I'm all that crazy."

The two teams are nearly exhausted, but the battle continues. Neither one will stop until the war is won, but the ropes remain firmly tied together across the width of the river. Then suddenly, there's a loud sound and both teams fall backwards as the **tension**[12] of the ropes is released. One set of kite ropes has finally broken and it belongs to the opposite team. It looks like Tamura's team is the winner of the *odako* battle for this year's festival!

---

[12]**tension:** the degree of tightness found when something is stretched between points

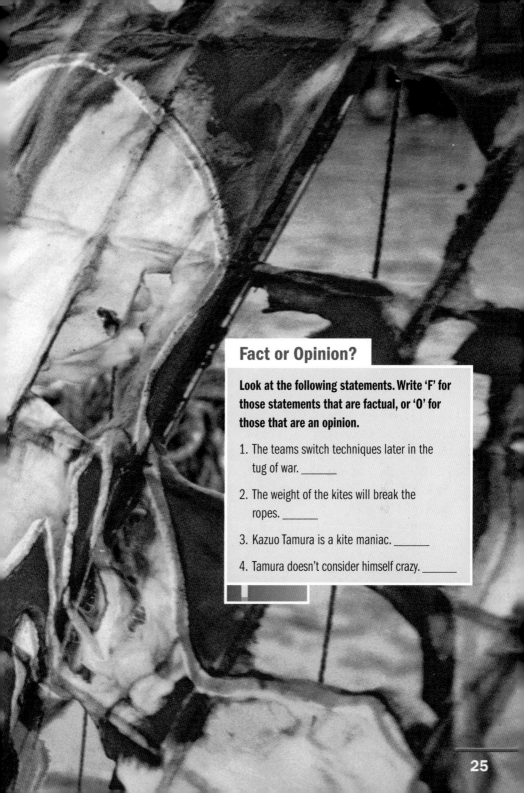

Fact or Opinion?

Look at the following statements. Write 'F' for those statements that are factual, or 'O' for those that are an opinion.

1. The teams switch techniques later in the tug of war. _____

2. The weight of the kites will break the ropes. _____

3. Kazuo Tamura is a kite maniac. _____

4. Tamura doesn't consider himself crazy. _____

So are the people of Shirone really Kite Crazy? Tamura certainly looked a little crazy when he finally had the opportunity to get into battle. But then, most of the residents of this village certainly seem to become very excited and passionate at this time of year. If it is some type of craziness, it is definitely not a dangerous one.

As the Great Kite Fight ends for another year, the competitors—both winners and losers—begin to clean up the damaged kites. In a good year every kite is destroyed, but the people of Shirone never seem to feel sorry that they are gone. They know that next year, the kites will live again, flying across the sky until 'Kite Craziness' is no more. For now, it appears that this unusual and interesting tradition is going strong, and there are no signs that the 'Kite Crazy' epidemic will disappear any time soon. In fact, among everyone who appears affected by it, no one seems to want to take the **cure**.[13]

---

[13]**cure:** an element which heals or betters an illness or disease

After You Read

1. Which word on page 4 means the 'state of someone'?
   A. activity
   B. condition
   C. enthusiast
   D. sleeplessness

2. According to Kazuo Tamura, which of the following does NOT describe 'kite crazy'?
   A. stealing a neighbor's kite
   B. caring about kites more than food
   C. imagining kites on the ceiling
   D. thinking about kites all the time

3. What is the writer's main purpose on page 7?
   A. to introduce specific people
   B. to explain the rules of the festival
   C. to give background information about the festival
   D. to show how kites can be dangerous

4. In paragraph 2 on page 11, 'them' in 'fly them' refers to:
   A. bombers
   B. jets
   C. *rokako*
   D. *odako*

5. What happens when a kite is captured?
   A. One team loses.
   B. The tug of war begins.
   C. The rope is cut.
   D. The competition is abandoned.

6. Extra points are awarded based upon the:
   A. length of the rope captured
   B. thrill of the fight
   C. time spent pulling
   D. size of the kite

7. According to the story, a team must have all of the following to win EXCEPT:
   A. a tough rope
   B. teamwork
   C. a good wind
   D. the most colorful kite

8. Why do the people of Shirone need a chance to go a little crazy?
   A. because there is no northern wind
   B. because they usually work very hard
   C. because the kite festival is completed
   D. because they are disappointed

9. A captured kite drops _____ the river.
   A. into
   B. down
   C. from
   D. on

10. What does the writer probably think about the *odako* battle on page 23?
    A. It's upsetting to watch.
    B. They are using minimum effort.
    C. It will have a tragic ending.
    D. It's an exciting event.

11. A suitable heading for page 24 is:
    A. Team Cuts Rope with Knife
    B. Madman Rushes into Festival
    C. Thrilling Championship Battle
    D. Yelling Wakes Neighbors

12. What conclusion does the writer make in paragraph 2 on page 27?
    A. Kite flying should become the national sport of Japan.
    B. The people of Shirone are proud of their kite tradition.
    C. No one can understand why the festival is popular.
    D. After the festival, competitors should go to the hospital.

Competing with Kites Around the World

KITE FIGHTS

Historians believe that people first started to fly kites thousands of years ago either in India, Afghanistan, or any other Asian country, depending upon the source. Somewhere in the early history of kite flying, the idea of having battles in the sky was born. One area well known for its fighter kites is India. There, kites called 'patang' or 'guda' are flown, and the rope used to fly them is coated with broken bits of glass. The winner is the one who is able to cut the ropes of all of the other competitors. Afghan fighter kites are much larger than their Indian cousins with some being up to five feet wide. They are usually constructed of different materials, and competitors use very lightweight paper for their creations.

The sport of kite fighting is also popular in such places as Japan, Korea, Thailand, parts of Europe, Cuba, and Brazil. Brazilian kites are often smaller constructions, but the competition between rivals is still just as enthusiastic. Part of the fun of kite fighting in Brazil involves cutting away someone else's kite and then stealing it. Trees and power lines in Brazilian cities are often full of lost or abandoned kites.

Score Chart for the 2008 Kitemaker's Competition

Entry Name	Flight 3	Bopper	Go Boy	Higher
Maker's Name	B. Okano	J. Diaz	L. Shen	S. Smith
Appearance Score out of 10	8.27	7.57	7.50	7.70
Flight Score out of 10	7.57	7.43	7.83	7.10
Construction Score out of 10	8.57	8.27	8.27	8.44
Design Score out of 10	7.82	8.23	7.50	7.33
Total Score out of 40	32.33	31.50	31.10	30.57

KITE-BUILDING COMPETITIONS

Kite-building competitions offer a totally different approach to the sport of kite flying. Each year, hundreds of festivals are held around the world in which people build their own kites and bring them to be judged by experts in the field. The American Kitefliers Association was formed over 40 years ago and today it is the largest such organization in the world with over 4,000 members in 35 countries. During the annual competitions, kites are judged on four characteristics: appearance, flight capability, construction technique, and design.

The kite's 'appearance' is simply a measure of how good the kite looks on the ground. The 'flight capability' category measures how well the flier is able to handle it. 'Construction technique' refers to how neatly and carefully the kite was made, and the 'design' category is a measure of how strong the structure of the kite is. Judges carefully assess all attributes when making their decisions. Although it's a fun sport, competitors take it very seriously and work extremely hard on their entries. You can research possible kite-building competitions in your area by going to the American Kitefliers Association website.

CD 2, Track 06

Word Count: 385
Time: _____

Vocabulary List

aggressive (17)
battle (2, 7, 9, 11, 12, 14, 23, 24, 27)
capture (3, 11, 12, 14, 23)
clash (3, 14, 24)
cling (3, 9, 12, 18)
crop (7)
cure (27)
enthusiastic (2, 4, 24)
epidemic (14, 27)
festival (2, 3, 7, 9, 11, 18, 21, 23, 24)
fighter jet (11)
heavy bomber (11)
kite (2, 3, 4, 7, 9, 11, 12, 14, 15, 17, 18, 21, 23, 24, 25, 27)
lord (7)
maniac (2, 24, 25)
parade (11)
passionate (4, 7, 27)
rival (3, 9, 12, 14, 23, 24)
tension (24)
tug of war (2, 3, 12, 14, 17, 23, 25)
twist (12, 14, 23)